PARIS

PARIS

A POEM

BY

HOPE MIRRLEES

FABER & FABER

Paris first published in 1920
by the Hogarth Press

This edition first published in 2020
by Faber & Faber Ltd
Bloomsbury House
74–77 Great Russell Street
London WC1B 3DA

Typeset by Typo•glyphix, Branston, Burton-on-Trent
Printed in the UK by TJ Books Limited, Padstow, Cornwall

A CIP record for this book
is available from the British Library

ISBN 978-0-571-35993-6

2 4 6 8 10 9 7 5 3

CONTENTS

FOREWORD

. . . behind the ramparts of the Louvre

Freud has dredged the river and, grinning horribly,
waves his garbage in a glare of electricity.

Taxis,

Taxis,

Taxis,

They moan and yell and squeak

If modernism was the language that lit up the early twentieth
century, it seems to me that Hope Mirrlees, aged twenty-six,
stepped into that light and flipped a switch of her own. In 1919,
when she set about writing the immersive polyphonic adventure
of a day and night walking through post-war Paris just after the
Armistice, it's possible that Mirrlees, in finding a form for the
multiple impressions that eventually became *Paris: A Poem*,
might even have astounded herself with her own audacity. It is
also a valuable historical document of a European city haunted
by the spectres of the war dead while the bereaved living go
about their every day.

No wonder Virginia and Leonard Woolf, who had set up the
Hogarth Press together, were keen to publish *Paris* in 1920.
Virginia Woolf even sewed by hand the 175 copies they printed
in their English home. It's exciting to think of the endeavour it
must have taken to visually lay out and print the typographical
effects and roaming line breaks – it's as if the poem itself is
strolling through the May Day demonstrations and street singers,

pausing to notice a red stud in the buttonhole of a gentleman's frock coat in Gambetta, then moving on to gaze at statues of nymphs with 'soft mouths'. Virginia Woolf must have enjoyed this splash of cosmopolitan life as their printing press (bought second-hand in 1917 for £41) rolled off the pages of Mirrlees's poem in their house in Richmond (then in Surrey).

> The sky is apricot;
> Against it there pass
> Across the Pont Solférino
> Fiacres and little people all black,

We could linger for a time to imagine this publishing moment at Hogarth House in interwar Britain. Perhaps the starlings were singing in the English mist, vegetables were being boiled to death in the kitchen, while in another room Mirrlees brought news of lesbian night-club 'gurls', advertisements in the métro for Dubonnet, cigarette papers and shoe polish – meanwhile the Seine, 'old egoist', is making its way to the sea and the ghosts of the dead mingle with children riding fairground horses. I can see Virginia being called to the table while rain drips in the garden, trapped (as she saw it) in sedate Richmond, glancing at these words:

> It is pleasant to sit on the Grands Boulevards—
>> They smell of
>> Cloacae
>> Hot indiarubber
>> Poudre de riz
>> Algerian tobacco

It's possible that Mirrlees was influenced by the concrete poetry of Apollinaire (she might have read his *Calligrammes* of 1918) and would never again, in her other writing, rise to the same level of linguistic bravado she achieved on that long walk in 1919. If this is my own view, it can be contested, and that is how it should be. Yet I believe it only gives *Paris* more allure. When Baudelaire and Rimbaud flâneured the same city, they were societally free to loiter in public space and observe metropolitan life with more ease and entitlement than Mirrlees could do – after all, female streetwalkers were apparently prostitutes and not poets. Living in Paris with her partner, the classicist Jane Ellen Harrison, Mirrlees had to find, technically, a formal arrangement to evoke simultaneous experience in the way that cubism had created a visual language to capture multiple points of view. At times she slows everything down to paint the mood of the city in three simple short lines:

> The wicked April moon
> The silence of *la grève*
> Rain

As the writer Francesca Wade points out in *Square Haunting* (2020), her superb literary history of five extraordinary women based in London between the wars (in which you will meet Hope Mirrlees, Virginia Woolf and Jane Harrison all figuring out how to invent a life that allows them to write and love freely), the British were never that keen on modernism. When the work of Matisse, Van Gogh, Gauguin and Cézanne was exhibited in London in 1910, Wade tells us how Virginia Woolf recorded the way it threw critics into 'paroxysms of rage and laughter'. Ten years later, when Mirrlees's poem was published, this atmosphere of cultural conservatism still prevailed. If there were not many readers for her unique early stretch of female modernist writing, it certainly paved the way for T. S. Eliot's *The Waste Land*, published in 1922.

My wish for the twenty-six-year-old Mirrlees is that she had been encouraged to fly higher and to continue with some of the innovations she had started to make manifest in *Paris*. All the same, you now hold in your hands the work of a fiercely independent, young and spirited, flawed and brilliant female writer. Mirrlees set the bar high in *Paris* and, with athletic grace, jumped over Victorian realism in her skirt and walking shoes, one hand on her hat to keep it from blowing into the Seine.

DEBORAH LEVY, 2020

PARIS

A
NOTRE DAME DE PARIS
EN RECONNAISSANCE
DES GRACES ACCORDEES

I want a holophrase

NORD-SUD

ZIG-ZAG
LION NOIR
CACAO BLOOKER

Black-figured vases in Etruscan tombs

RUE DU BAC (DUBONNET)
SOLFERINO (DUBONNET)
CHAMBRE DES DEPUTES

Brekekekek coax coax we are passing under the Seine

DUBONNET

The Scarlet Woman shouting BYRRH and deafening
St. John at Patmos

Vous descendez Madame?

QUI SOUVENT SE PESE BIEN SE CONNAIT
QUI BIEN SE CONNAIT BIEN SE PORTE

CONCORDE

I can't
I must go slowly

(3)

The   Tuileries   are   in   a   trance

because   the   painters   have

stared   at   them   so   long

Little boys in black overalls whose hands, sticky with play, are like the newly furled leaves of the horse-chestnuts ride round and round on wooden horses till their heads turn.

> Pigeons perch on statues
> And are turned to stone.

Le départ pour Cythère.

> These nymphs are harmless,
> Fear not their soft mouths—
> Some Pasteur made the Gauls immune
> Against the bite of Nymphs . . . look

Gambetta
A red stud in the button-hole of his frock-coat
The obscene conjugal *tutoiment*
Mais c'est logique.

The Esprit Français is leaning over him,
Whispering

Secrets
exquisite   significant
fade   plastic

Of the XIIIth Duchess of Alba
Long long as the Eiffel Tower
Fathoms deep in haschich
With languid compelling finger
Pointing invisible Magi
To a little white Maltese:

The back-ground gray and olive-green
Like le Midi, the Louvre, la Seine. . . .

Of ivory paper-knives, a lion carved on the handle,
Lysistrata had one, but the workmanship of these is
Empire. . . .

Of . . .

I see the Arc de Triomphe,
Square and shadowy like Julius Cæsar's dreams:

Scorn the laws of solid geometry,

Step boldly into the wall of the Salle Caillebotte

And on and on . . .

I hate the Etoile
The Bois bores me:

Tortoises with gem-encrusted carapace

A Roman boy picking a thorn out of his foot

A flock of discalceated Madame Récamiers
Moaning for the Chateaubriand *de nos jours.*

And yet . . . quite near

Saunters the ancient rue Saint-Honoré
Shabby and indifferent, as a Grand Seigneur from Brit-
tany

An Auvergnat, all the mountains of Auvergne in
every chestnut that he sells. . . .

Paris is a huge home-sick peasant,
He carries a thousand villages in his heart.

Hidden courts
With fauns in very low-relief piping among lotuses
And creepers grown on trellises
Are secret valleys where little gods are born.

One often hears a cock
Do do do mi i i

He cannot sing of towns—
Old Hesiod's ghost with leisure to be melancholy
Amid the timeless idleness of Acheron
Yearning for 'Works and Days' . . . hark!

The lovely Spirit of the Year
Is stiff and stark

Laid out in acres of brown fields,

The crisp, straight lines of his archaic drapery
Well chiselled by the plough . . .

And there are pretty things—
Children hung with amulets
Playing at *Pigeon vole*,
Red roofs,
Blue smocks,
And jolly saints . . .

AU
BON MARCHE
ACTUELLEMENT
TOILETTES
PRINTANIERES

The jeunesse dorée of the sycamores.

In the Churches during Lent Christ and the Saints
are shrouded in mauve veils.

Far away in gardens
Crocuses,
Chionodoxa, the Princess in a Serbian fairy-tale,
Then
The goldsmith's chef d'œuvre—lily of the valley,
Soon

Dog-roses will stare at gypsies, wanes, and pilgrimages

All the time
Scentless Lyons' roses,
Icy,
Plastic,
Named after wives of Mayors. . . .

Did Ingres paint a portrait of Madame Jacquemart André?

In the Louvre
The Pietà of Avignon,
L'Olympe,
Giles,
Mantegna's Seven Deadly Sins,
The Chardins;

They arise, serene and unetiolated, one by one from their subterranean sleep of five long years.

Like Duncan they slept well.

President Wilson grins like a dog and runs about the city, sniffing with innocent enjoyment the diluvial urine of Gargantua.

The poplar buds are golden chrysalids;
The Ballet of green Butterflies
Will soon begin.

During the cyclic Grand Guignol of Catholicism
Shrieks,
Lacerations,
Bloody sweat—
Le petit Jésus fait pipi.

Lilac

SPRING IS SOLOMON'S LITTLE SISTER; SHE HAS NO
BREASTS.

LAIT SUPERIEUR
DE LA
FERME DE RAMBOUILLET

ICI ON CONSULTE
LE BOTTIN

CHARCUTERIE
COMESTIBLES DE IRE CHOIX

APERITIFS

ALIMENTS DIABETIQUES
DEUIL EN 24 HEURES

Messieursetdames

Little temples of Mercury;
The circumference of their *templum*
A nice sense of scale,

A golden drop of Harpagon's blood,
     Preserve from impious widening.

Great bunches of lilac among syphons, vermouth,
Bocks, tobacco.

Messieursetdames

NE FERMEZ PAS LA PORTE
S. V. P
LE PRIMUS S'EN CHARGERA

At marble tables sit ouvriers in blue linen suits discuss-
ing:
          La journée de huit heures,
          Whether Landru is a Sadist,
          The learned seal at the Nouveau Cirque
               Cottin. . . .

Echoes of Bossuet chanting dead queens.

          méticuleux
          bélligerants
          hebdomadaire
          immonde

          The Roman Legions
               Wingèd
               Invisible
          Fight their last fight in Gaul.

The ghost of Père Lachaise
Is walking the streets,
He is draped in a black curtain embroidered with the
letter H,
He is hung with paper wreaths,
He is beautiful and horrible and the close friend of
Rousseau, the official of the Douane.

The unities are smashed,
The stage is thick with corpses. . . .

Kind clever *gaillards*
Their *eidola* in hideous frames inset with the brass
motto

MORT AU CHAMP D'HONNEUR;

And little widows moaning
Le pauvre grand!
Le pauvre grand!

And petites bourgeoises with tight lips and strident
voices are counting out the change and saying *Messieursetdames* and their hearts are the ruined province
of Picardie. . . .

They are not like us, who, ghoul-like, bury our friends
a score of times before they're dead but—

Never never again will the Marne
Flow between happy banks.

It is pleasant to sit on the Grand Boulevards—
They smell of

                    Cloacæ
                  Hot indiarubber
                   Poudre de riz
                 Algerian tobacco

Monsieur Jourdain in the blue and red of the Zouaves
        Is premier danseur in the Ballet Turque
                    'Ya bon!
                  Mamamouchi

YANKEES—"and say besides that in Aleppo once . . ."

Many a *Mardi Gras* and *Carême Prenant* of the
Peace Carnival;

                   Crape veils,
Mouths pursed up with lip-salve as if they had just said:
                 Cho - co - lat . . .
          "Elles se balancent sur les hanches."

                  Lizard-eyes,
                 Assyrian beards,
               Boots with cloth tops—

The tart little race, whose brain, the Arabs said, was
one of the three perches of the Spirit of God.

Ouiouioui, c'esi passionnant—on en a pour son argent.
      Le fromage n'est pas un plat logique.

A a a a a oui c'est un délicieux garçon
Il me semble que toute femme sincère doit se retrouver
en Anna Karénine.

Never the catalepsy of the Teuton
What time
Subaqueous
Cell on cell
Experience
Very slowly
Is forming up
Into something beautiful—awful—huge

The coming to .   .   .   .   .   .
Thick halting speech—the curse of vastness.

The first of May
T
h
e
r
e
i
s
n
o
l
i
l
y
o
f

t
h
e

v
a
l
l
e
y

There was a ritual fight for her sweet body
    Between two virgins—Mary and the moon

    The wicked April moon.

     The silence of *la grève*

      Rain

    The Louvre is melting into mist

     It will soon be transparent
And through it will glimmer the mysterious island
gardens of the Place du Carrousel.

The Seine, old egotist, meanders imperturbably to-
                           wards the sea,

Ruminating on weeds and rain . . .
   If through his sluggish watery sleep come dreams
     They are the blue ghosts of king-fishers.

The Eiffel Tower is two dimensional,
Etched on thick white paper.

Poilus in wedgwood blue with bundles *Terre de Sienne*
are camping round the gray sphinx of the Tuileries.
They look as if a war-artist were making a sketch of
them in chalks, to be 'edited' in the Rue des Pyram-
ides at 10 francs a copy.

Désœuvrement,
Apprehension;
Vronsky and Anna
Starting up in separate beds in a cold sweat
Reading calamity in the same dream
Of a gigantic sinister mujik. . . .

Whatever happens, some day it will look beautiful:
Clio is a great French painter,
She walks upon the waters and they are still.
Shadrach, Meshach, and Abednego stand motionless
and plastic mid the flames.

Manet's *Massacres des Jours de Juin*,
David's *Prise de la Bastille*,
Poussin's *Fronde*,

Hang in a quiet gallery.

All this time the Virgin has not been idle;
The windows of les Galéries Lafayette, le Bon Marché,
la Samaritaine,

Hold holy bait,
Waxen Pandoras in white veils and ties of her own
decking;
Catéchisme de Persévérance,
The decrees of the Seven Œcumenical Councils re-
duced to the *format* of the *Bibliothèque Rose*,
Première Communion,
(Prometheus has swallowed the bait)
Petits Lycéens,
Por-no-gra-phie,
Charming pigmy brides,
Little Saint Hugh avenged—

THE CHILDREN EAT THE JEW.

PHOTO MIDGET

Heigh ho!
I wade knee-deep in dreams—

Heavy sweet going
As through a field of hay in Périgord.

The Louvre, the Ritz, the Palais-Royale, the Hôtel
de Ville

Are light and frail
Plaster pavilions of pleasure
Set up to serve the ten days junketing
Of citizens in masks and dominoes
A l'occasion du marriage de Monseigneur le Dauphin.

From the top floor of an old Hôtel,
Tranced,
I gaze down at the narrow rue de Beaune.
Hawkers chant their wares liturgically:
Hatless women in black shawls
Carry long loaves—Triptolemos in swaddling clothes:
Workmen in pale blue:
Barrows of vegetables:
Busy dogs:
They come and go.
They are very small.

Stories. . . .

The lost romance
Penned by some Ovid, an unwilling thrall
In Fairyland,
No one knows its name;
It was the guild-secret of the Italian painters.
They spent their lives in illustrating it. . . .

The Chinese village in a genius's mind. . . .

Little funny things ceaselessly happening.

In the Ile Saint-Louis, in the rue Saint Antoine, in
the Place des Vosges
The Seventeenth Century lies exquisitely dying. . . .

Hu s s s h

dim - - in - - u - en - do. *ppp*

In the parish of Saint Thomas d'Aquin there is
an alley called l'impasse des Deux Anges.

Houses with rows of impassive windows;

They are like blind dogs
The only things that they can see are ghosts.

Hark to the small dry voice
As of an old nun chanting Masses
For the soul of a brother killed at Sebastopol. . . .

MOLIERE

EST MORT

DANS CETTE MAISON

LE 17 FEVRIER 1673

VOLTAIRE

EST MORT

DANS CETTE MAISON

LE 30 MAI 1778

(18)

CHATEAUBRIAND
EST MORT
DANS CETTE MAISON
LE 4 JUILLET 1848

That is not all,
Paradise cannot hold for long the famous dead
of Paris. . . .

There are les Champs Elysées!

Sainte-Beuve, a tight bouquet in his hand for Madame
Victor-Hugo,
Passes on the Pont-Neuf the duc de la Rochefoucauld
With a superbly leisurely gait
Making for the *salon d'automne*
Of Madame de Lafayette;

They cannot see each other.

Il fait lourd,
The dreams have reached my waist.

We went to Benediction in Notre-Dame-des-Champs,
Droning. . . droning. . . droning.
The Virgin sits in her garden;
She wears the blue habit and the wingèd linen head-
dress of the nuns of Saint Vincent de Paul.
The Holy Ghost coos in his dove-cot.
The Seven Stages of the Cross are cut in box,

Lilies bloom, blue, green, and pink,
　The bulbs were votive offerings
　　From a converted Jap.
　　An angelic troubadour
　　　Sings her songs
　　Of little venial sins.
Upon the wall of sunset-sky wasps never fret
　　The plums of Paradise.

　　　La Liberté La Presse!
　　　La Liberté La Presse!

The sun is sinking behind le Petit-Palais.
In the Algerian desert they are shouting the Koran.

　　　La Liberté La Presse!

　　The sky is apricot;
　　Against it there pass
　　Across the Pont Solférino
Fiacres and little people all black,

　　Flies nibbling the celestial apricot—
That one with broad-brimmed hat and tippeted pelisse
　　　　　　　　　must be a priest.

They are black and two-dimensional and look like silhouettes of Louis-Philippe citizens.

All down the Quais the bouquinistes shut their green boxes.

From the VIIme arrondissement
Night like a vampire
Sucks all colour, all sound.

The winds are sleeping in their Hyperbórean cave;

The narrow streets bend proudly to the stars;

From time to time a taxi hoots like an owl.

But behind the ramparts of the Louvre

Freud has dredged the river and, grinning horribly,
waves his garbage in a glare of electricity.

Taxis,
Taxis,
Taxis,

They moan and yell and squeak
Like a thousand tom-cats in rut.

The whores like lions are seeking their meat from God:

An English padre tilts with the Moulin Rouge:

Crotchets and quavers have the heads of niggers and
they writhe in obscene syncopation:

Toutes les cartes marchent avec une allumette!

A hundred lenses refracting the Masque of the Seven
Deadly Sins for American astigmatism:

"*I dont like the gurls of the night-club—they love
women.*"

Toutes les cartes marchent avec une allumette!

DAWN

Verlaine's bed-time . . . Alchemy
Absynthe,
Algerian tobacco,
Talk, talk, talk,
Manuring the white violets of the moon.

The President of the Republic lies in bed beside his wife, and it may be at this very moment . . .

In the Abbaye of Port-Royal babies are being born,

Perhaps someone who cannot sleep is reading *le Crime et le Châtiment*.

The sun is rising,
Soon les Halles will open,
The sky is saffron behind the two towers of Nôtre-Dame.

JE VOUS SALUE PARIS PLEIN DE GRACE.

*

*

*

*　　*

*　　*

3 Rue de Beaune
Paris
Spring　1919

NOTES

P.I. *Nord-Sud*, one of the underground railways of Paris. *Dubonnet*, *Zig-zag*, *Lion Noir*, *Cacao Blooker* are posters. *Rue du Bac*, etc. are names of stations.

P.II. "It is pleasant to sit on the Grands Boulevards" to page 13 "the curse of vastness" is a description of the Grands Boulevards.

P.I3. "The first of May, there is no lily of the valley." On May 1, the *Mois de Marie*, lily of the valley is normally sold in all the streets of Paris; but on May 1, 1919, the day of the general strike, no lily of the valley was offered for sale.

P.I4. The April moon, *la lune rousse*, is supposed to have a malign influence on vegetation.

P.I5. "The windows of les Galéries Lafayette, etc." During Lent life-size wax dolls, dressed like candidates for Première Communion, are exposed in the windows of the big shops.

P.22. The Abbaye de Port-Royal is now a maternity hospital.

COMMENTARY

The page and line numbers have been updated to relate to this edition of *Paris*.

P.2.

Dedication   'To Our Lady of Paris in recognition of graces granted'. 'Our Lady of Paris' is both the Virgin Mary and the great cathedral dedicated to her on the Ile-de-la-Cité, at the centre of Paris, with an echo of the prayer 'Ave Maria, gratia plena' ('Hail Mary, full of grace' – see p. 22, l. 15). The frame suggests that of a votive plaque such as might be hung in a church. From the outset, Paris is addressed as a woman.

P.3.

1   'holophrase', a single word standing for a phrase, sentence or complex of ideas, and according to Jane Harrison (JH) character-istic of an early stage of language development (*Themis* 473–5). 'I want' can also mean 'I lack'. 'Holophrase' puns on 'hollow phrase'.

2   Métro line from Montparnasse to Montmartre, now line 12.

3–6   Brand names on métro posters: 'Zig-Zag', type of cigarette paper, advertised with the head of a 'Zouave', an Algerian soldier (and anticipating the poem's zig-zag direction through the city); 'Lion Noir' (black lion), a brand of shoe polish; 'Cacao Blooker', Dutch make of drinking chocolate. These introduce themes of empire and of *négritude* (blackness), further linked with 'Black-figured vases' (550–480 BC), found in Etruscan burial chambers.

7–9   'Rue du Bac', 'Solférino' and 'Chambre des Députés' (now 'Assemblée Nationale'), the three most northerly stations on the Nord-Sud line south of the river (rue du Bac is next to rue de Beaune, where Hope Mirrlees [HM] lived while writing the poem). 'Solférino', named for a French victory over Austria in Italy (1859). From 1832, the Chambre des Députés was the French lower house of government. 'Dubonnet', brand of fortified wine advertised in métro tunnels, HM's curved brackets suggesting the walls of the métro on which the posters appeared.

10   'Brekekekek coax coax', chorus of Aristophanes' *The Frogs* (405 BC) in the underworld (also suggesting rattling wooden carriages in the métro). 'Frogs', British slang for the French, used in letters between HM and JH.

12–13   'The Scarlet Woman' appears to St John on the Greek island of Patmos (Revelation 17.3–6). 'Byrrh', another fortified wine, advertised with a poster of a woman dressed in scarlet, playing a drum and shouting (see Cocteau 49, 38 for 'BYRRH' and St John as witness). In the Hogarth edition, 'St.' is inserted before 'John' by Virginia Woolf's hand on 160 copies.

14   'Are you getting off here, madame?' standard polite phrase for making one's own way off a crowded métro car or bus.

15–16   'Those who weigh themselves [up] often, know themselves well. Those who know themselves well, stay healthy', motto on station scales.

17   The speaker alights at the first station north of the river: Place de la Concorde, a huge square on the Right Bank, formerly used for royal events, the guillotine during the revolution, etc. 'Concorde' means 'agreement', introducing the theme of the peace process (MacMillan, passim).

P.4.

1–3   The spaced-out layout of these lines imitates that of the Tuileries gardens, with gaps left for the basins on the central axis at either end. The poem slows down, changing direction from south > north (vertical movement on the page) to west > east (horizontal).

4–7   The little boys riding on a carousel in the Tuileries (out of use during World War I) become soldiers, their hands sticky from the mud of the trenches (anticipates p. 7, ll. 5–8; p. 15, ll. 3–4).

8–10   The pigeons appear to be joined to the statues in the Tuileries, while the statues look 'two-dimensional' (p. 15, l. 1; p. 20, l. 20). One, looking over her shoulder, suggests Watteau's *Le Départ pour Cythère* (properly, *L'Embarcation pour Cythère*, 1717, in the Louvre), in which those leaving for Cytherea (the island of Venus) look back.

11–15   Some statues are of nymphs. Louis Pasteur (1822–95) developed a vaccine against rabies (Sacha Guitry's play *Pasteur* was running in Paris in early 1919. A métro station on the Nord-Sud line had been named after him). 'Gauls', the French, as warriors or soldiers. The Nymphs' soft mouths also suggest female genitals ('nymphae', labia minora); their 'bite' may refer to venereal disease.

15–20   Leon Gambetta, national hero and Minister for War during the German siege of Paris, announced the Third Republic in September 1870 (in the presence of the 1919 Prime Minister Georges Clemençeau – the first buried reference to him). Gambetta's statue in a frock coat (now in the square Edouar-Vailant, 20éme) then stood at the base of a seventy-five-foot monumental pyramid in front of the Louvre, with a winged 'Genius of France' leaning over him. HM imagines a red stud (his *legion d'honneur* rosette) in a button-hole (*boutonnière* is slang for anus), suggesting a possible intimacy between these two figures.

17   *tutoiement*, an intimate form of address (*tu*) employed by couples.

18   *'But it makes sense.'*

19   Esprit Français, 'Spirit of France'. The winged 'Genius' on the Gambetta monument.

1–3 'Secrets', defined by four terms set in a square that play between English and French senses: 'exquisite' (Fr. *exquis*); 'significant' (Fr. *significatif*); 'fade', a verb in English, an adjective in French meaning tasteless or insipid; 'plastic' (*plastique*), malleable, moulded, flowing, often applied to sculpture or the visual arts, a favourite word for HM (see p. 8, l. 4; p. 15, l. 17; HM's novel *Madeleine*, vii).

4–11 (Exquisite / significant secrets) Of . . . Goya's painting of the Duchess of Alba (1795, near the end of the war between France, Germany and Spain) depicts her as tall and slender, a pyramid, resembling both the Eiffel Tower and Gambetta's monument. Red ribbons in her hair and on her dress echo his red stud. She seems drugged, and, like him, is pointing, in her case to a small (Maltese) dog at her feet, as if directing the Magi to the infant Jesus at Epiphany. HM and JH may have seen this painting in Madrid in 1916; Goya was fashionable with the French avant-garde.

12 (Significant / plastic secrets) Of . . . On the top of the Gambetta monument was a figure of Democracy riding on a lion. *Lysistrata*, heroine of a play by Aristophanes (411 BC), persuaded the women of Athens to end the war with Sparta by going on sexual strike. The play was staged at the Marigny Theatre, and another play inspired by it, *La grève des femmes*, was also running in Paris in spring 1919.

15 ('Fade' or fading secrets) Of . . .

16–17 From the Place du Carrousel, the Arc de Triomphe is visible at the far end of the Champs Elysées. Caesar (whose statue stands in the Tuileries) scorns dreams in Shakespeare's play.

19 Salle Caillebotte, room in the Musée du Luxembourg, hung with French Impressionist paintings. The painter Gustave

Caillebotte's unique collection of these was at first refused by the French government, but from 1896 most of them were on display.

20   The journey through Paris continues.

21–2   'The Etoile', the *place* at the top of the Champs Elysées, at the centre of the fashionable west side, named 'etoile' (star) because twelve avenues radiated from it. 'The Bois' (Bois de Boulogne), public park at its western edge.

P.6.

1   In J-K. Huysmans' decadent novel *A Rebours* (1884), Des Esseintes has the shell of a living tortoise encrusted with jewels.

2   'Spinario', Roman statue in bronze (first century BC) in the Museo dei Conservatori in Rome. Renaissance copies abound, some in the Louvre.

3–4   Juliette Récamier, famous beauty, and lover of the poet Chateaubriand (p. 19, l. 1). 'Discalceated', a rare word for 'bare-footed', as she appears in a portrait (1800) by Jacques-Louis David (p. 15, l. 19), in the Louvre. *De nos jours*, of our time.

6–7   'Saunters' suggests the *flâneur*, stroller or wanderer, a characteristic Parisian type; 'rue Saint-Honoré', old street meandering from east to west parallel with the river (Chateaubriand lived at no. 374). 'Grand Seigneur', a great lord. Brittany, the westernmost region of France, introduces a tour of the provinces.

8   Auvergnat, hot chestnut-seller, native of the Auvergne, the mountainous area of central France. Celtic Brittany and the Gallic Auvergne represent old traditional French stock. Many nineteenth-century Parisians came from Brittany and central France (Higonnet 77).

10–15   Paris was often pictured as a city of peasants, and its *quartiers* thought of as villages, especially by the Surrealists (see

Louis Aragon's later *Le Paysan de Paris*, 1926). Many Paris houses have large gates, providing glimpses of 'Hidden courts' decorated with classical figures such as 'putti', though the 'little gods' could be the city's artists, musicians and writers.

16   The Gallic cock is a national symbol. The cock wakens the farmer, usually banishing ghosts, though here it becomes the ghost of Hesiod, an early Greek poet who 'sang' (as the cock does) of country life in his *Works and Days* (both denied to the dead). 'Acheron' was one of the four rivers of the classical underworld / afterlife.

22   That is, peace; also the 'Eniautos Daimon', whose birth and death correspond to seasonal change, the central theme of JH's *Themis*.

P.7.

1–3   The Spirit of the Year is laid out, corpse-like, in fields whose ploughed furrows ('nos sillons') suggest the fluted drapery of archaic Greek statues, as well as the trenches of World War I.

5–8   Children hung with amulets (good luck charms, to protect from danger) are also reincarnated soldiers (as at p. 4, l. 4; see Cocteau 41). *Pigeon vole* (literally, 'pigeon, fly'), children's game that also recalls extensive use of pigeons to carry military information in World War I. Red and blue are the colours of Paris, and the blue smocks recall the blue uniforms of French soldiers (as at p. 15, l. 3).

10–14   'At Bon Marche, Spring Outfits Available Now'. Bon Marché, large department store in the rue de Babylone, subject of Zola's 1883 novel, *Au Bonheur des Dames* (*Ladies' Paradise*) (Higonnet 200).

15   'jeunesse dorée', gilded youth, used of wealthy, spoilt young people, but also of the buds on the sycamore trees.

(30)

16–17   Mauve or purple is the ritual colour used in Lent.

19–20   'Crocuses / Chionodoxa', flower of early spring. Crocuses are frequently mauve. Blue or white chionodoxa, meaning 'glory of the snow', a suitable name for a fairy-tale princess. Serbia also recalls the assassination of the Archduke at Sarajevo that triggered World War I.

22–4   'chef d'oeuvre', masterpiece. The floral pageant runs from crocuses, to lily of the valley sold on 1 May (see p. 13, ll. 11–26; p. 14, ll. 1–9) to the dog-roses of early summer. The dog-roses reverse the gaze of painters (p. 4, ll. 2–3) by watching the annual pilgrimage of gypsies to Saintes-Maries-de-la-Mer in the Camargue on 23–25 May; 'wanes', an unusual spelling of 'wains', or wagons. 'Charles's wain', another name for the Great Bear (see p. 22, l. 16).

P.8.

2–5   'Roses from Lyons', a major city, south-east of Paris. Unlike dog-roses, they are 'scentless' (*fade?*), yet 'plastic', or moulded. In 1913 Joseph Pernet-Ducher named a hybrid tea-rose 'Mme Edouard Herriot' after the wife of the then mayor of Lyons.

6–7   The French painter J. A. D. Ingres (1780–1867) apparently did not paint Mme Nélie Jacquemart-André (1841–1912), herself a portrait painter and art collector. Her home became the Musée Jacquemart-André at 158, Blvd. Haussmann.

8–13   In February 1919, paintings stored underground for safety were rehung in the Louvre, including the fifteenth-century *Pietà* from Villeneuve-les-Avignon; Edouard Manet's controversial nude, *Olympia* (1863), first displayed in 1907 after a campaign by Georges Clemençeau (on Manet, see p. 15, l. 18); 'Gil[l]es', Watteau's painting of a Pierrot (1718–19); 'Mantegna's Seven Deadly Sins', properly *Minerva Chasing the Vices from the Garden of*

Virtue (ca. 1502); J.-B.-S Chardin (1699–1779) specialised in domestic scenes and still life.

14–16   'Unetiolated', not pale from being stored in a dark, underground place. Shakespeare's Macbeth claims of his murdered victim, 'Duncan is in his grave. / After life's fitful fever, he sleeps well' (III.ii.22–3). The paintings implicitly contrast with dead soldiers, who cannot be resurrected, and may not 'sleep well'.

17–19   Greeted rapturously as 'Wilson le Juste' on his arrival in Paris for the peace talks, President Woodrow Wilson brought his fourteen-point plan, which promised more than it could deliver (MacMillan 3–20). 'Gargantua', figuring old Europe, was an anarchic giant, and title character of Rabelais' fantasy (1534–5); his urine was indeed 'diluvial', or flood-like (the French describe heavy rain as 'pluie diluvienne'). Wilson's 'innocent enjoyment' appeared to Clemençeau 'pathetic naiveté' (MacMillan 23).

20   'chrysalids', cocoons or pupae that will release butterflies (as the buds release leaves).

P.9.

1   Easter (Good Friday, 18 April 1919). 'Grand Guignol' ('blood and guts') was a violent, sensational type of melodrama performed at the Grand Guignol theatre in Montmartre (see p. 11, ll. 7–8).

3   Ritual self-flagellation was a regular feature of Good Friday processions.

5   Little Jesus does a pee-pee. 'Le petit jésus', pretty child, can also be slang for a boy prostitute.

6   Lilac flowers near the end of Lent, its colour echoing that of the church draperies (p. 7, l. 17; p. 10, l. 3).

7–8   *Song of Solomon* 8.8: 'We have a little sister, and she has no breasts' (see also *Song of Soloman* 2.11–12 for its evocation of spring).

9–11   'Quality milk from the Rambouillet farm', the first of a series of street signs. Rambouillet, a small town south-west of Paris, where Louis XVI created the Ferme de Rambouillet, the Queen's dairy, for Marie-Antoinette. The Hôtel Rambouillet (in Paris) was the first and greatest French *salon* (see HM' s novel *Madeleine*, chapter IX).

12–13   'The telephone directory can be consulted here'.

14–15   'Delicatessen, for best quality cold cuts'.

16–17   'Pre-meal drinks' / 'Food for diabetics' (literally, 'diabetic food').

18   'Your clothes dyed black in 24 hours' (literally, 'mourning in 24 hours'). This and the previous sign are examples of 'catachresis', the application of a term to something it does not properly denote. According to MacMillan (26–7), in the Paris of 1919 'almost every other woman wore mourning'.

19   'Gentlemen-and-ladies', written thus to reflect its pronunciation on the streets by waiters, etc. (see p. 10, l. 5; p. 11, ll. 17–18).

20–2   A Roman temple to Mercury, the winged messenger of the gods, once stood on Montmartre, where the cathedral of the Sacré Coeur had recently been completed (dedicated October 1919). *Templum* is Latin for a sacred space, but 'Little temples' might refer to the circular kiosks on the boulevards or even open-air urinals (*pissoirs*).

P.10.

1–2   Harpagon is *The Miser* of Molière's play (1668), who regards his money as his blood (see V.iii). East of the Sacré Coeur (sacred heart) is the rue de la Goutte d'Or (golden drop), its name derived from the wealth of the vineyards formerly on that site, so the 'golden drop of Harpagon's blood' (money) may be contrasted with the blood of the Sacred Heart. But if the 'golden drop' is urine (as at p. 8, ll. 18–19), this might refer to the homosexual activities for which the *pissoirs* had been notorious since the eighteenth century.

3–4 In a typical bar-tabac: vermouth is a type of aperitif; bocks are glasses of beer.

6–8 'Don't close the door, please, the Primus [a compressed air device] will take care of it.'

9 ouvriers: workmen, who discuss recent news items.

10 'the eight-hour day', demanded by the workers and voted on by the government on 17 and 23 April, but the difficulties of implementing it resulted in a general strike on 1 May (p. 13, ll. 11–26; p. 14, ll. 1–9; p. 14, l. 13; Hausser 723, 724).

11 Henri Landru was a serial killer. The police investigated his activities from April to May 1919.

12 According to a programme for 2 May 1919, the learned seal was 'Bichette' and her trainer was Capitaine Juge; the Nouveau Cirque was at 251, rue Saint-Honoré.

13 On 19 February, the anarchist Emile Cottin attempted to assassinate Georges Clemençeau, chairman of the Peace Conference (see notes on p. 4, ll. 15–20; p. 8, ll. 8–13; Hausser 715; MacMillan 150–1). Cottin was condemned to death in March, but reprieved. His name suggests that of the Abbé Charles Cotin (1604–82), habitué of the Hôtel Rambouillet (see *Madeleine*, 55).

14 Jacques Benigne Bossuet (1624–1704), bishop and preacher, famous for his funeral sermons, particularly that on Henrietta Maria, Charles I's queen ('chanting dead queens').

15–18 Four adjectives probably refer to the previous discussion: *méticuleux*, punctilious, scrupulous (Cottin?); *bélligerants*, aggressive, warlike (the German, according to the newpapers?); *hebdomadaire*, weekly (of the eight-hour day); *immonde*, monstrous, foul (Landru?).

19–22   The Roman Legions in their winged helmets could be seen as invaders of Gaul (France) (like the defeated Germans) or else as France's departing allies.

P.11.

1–3   Père Lachaise, third of the trio of seventeenth-century clerics, was the Jesuit confessor of Louis XIV and gave his name to Paris's most famous cemetery. He appears wearing a curtain (introducing the theatre of war), embroidered with the letter H (pronounced 'ash' in French, and so suggesting the words of the English funeral service, 'Dust to dust, and ashes to ashes') – in French *hache* also means axe.

6   Henri Rousseau (1844–1910), known as the Douanier (customs officer), was a French 'Sunday' painter whose paintings ('beautiful and horrible') were admired by the avant-garde, especially after Picasso gave a famous dinner for him (1908). HM may have known his painting *La Guerre* (1894).

7–8   The artistic representation of violent events now dominates the poem. World War 1 failed conspicuously to conform to any rules, let alone the unities of time, place and action required of classical tragedy; it was closer to Grand Guignol (p. 9, l. 1), which left 'The stage . . . thick with corpses'.

9   *gaillards*, big, strapping fellows.

10   *eidola*, (Greek) ghosts, spirits, images.

12   Killed in action (literally, 'dead on the field of honour').

14–15   'The poor man!'

16   'petites bourgeoises', middle-class women, collecting money for war victims (p. 9, l. 19; p. 10, l. 5). Picardie is a province in

northern France, site of much of the fighting in World War I.

20   ghoul-like, ghouls rob graves and eat corpses.

22–3   The battle of the Marne (1914) was the worst battle of World War I for the French in terms of losses, their army being almost cut off by German forces in eastern France. The river Marne flows westwards to join the Seine near Paris, where its banks were lined with 'guingettes', dance halls, popular at weekends.

24   'The Grand[s] Boulevards', a series of wide streets running north of the rue Saint-Honoré, on an east-west axis, lined with theatres and cinemas – a favourite Sunday afternoon walk (the poem seems to zig-zag east from Concorde to the Louvre, west along the rue Saint-Honoré towards the Madeleine, then east along the Grands Boulevards). From here to p. 13, l. 10 is a description of the Grands Boulevards.

P.12.

1–4   'Cloacae' (Latin), sewers below the boulevards; 'Hot india-rubber', from car tyres – by 1914, there were 25,000 cars in Paris (Higonnet 187); 'Poudre de riz', face powder; 'Algerian tobacco' (see p. 22, l. 5) was cheap – themes of empire and racial alterity re-appear, picking up on 'Zig-Zag' (p. 3, l. 3), cigarette papers rolled around Algerian tobacco and joints.

5–6   'Monsieur Jourdain', *Le Bourgeois Gentilhomme* of Molière's play (1670), dresses up and joins in a Turkish dance in order to become a 'Mamamouchi'. He is here pictured in the blue and red uniform of the French Algerian army, the Zouaves. '[P]remier danseur', chief soloist; 'Ballet Turque' [turc], Turkish ballet.

7   'Dat's good!', the slogan advertising the breakfast food, 'Banania', on a famous poster showing a Senegalese rifleman sitting under a palm tree.

9   'YANKEES', Americans, either in Paris for the Peace Conference,

(36)

or staying on after World War I. African-Americans often settled in Montmartre, where they found a tolerant atmosphere (Higonnet 340–2). '[A]nd say besides . . .', Shakespeare's Moor of Venice, Othello, just before his suicide, remembers how he summarily executed a Turk who had 'Beat a Venetian, and traduced the State' (V.ii.354 – thus picking up the Turkish theme).

10–11 *Mardi gras*, Shrove Tuesday, the last day before Lent, the period of forty days fasting before Easter; *Carême Prenant*, Shrovetide, the days before the start of Lent, a period of merry-making or 'Carnival', before the fast; here linked with the Peace Conference, as a celebration before repentance and deprivation.

12–14 Crêpes (Shrovetide pancake) become 'crape', thin black mourning veils; *Cho-co-lat*, Cho-co-late – the second 'o' is long, and emphasised in French pronunciation.

15 'The women rock themselves backwards and forwards on their haunches.'

17 Square-cut beards, as portrayed on Assyrian statues.

19 Tart: sharp, acid; 'The tart little race' might be the Armenians, victims of Turkish massacres, who sent a special delegation to the Peace Conference (MacMillan 377).

21–2 'Yesyesyes, isn't it exciting – and such good value for money. Cheese isn't a rational dish' (see p. 4, l. 18).

23–5 'A-a-ah yes, he's a charming boy. / I think every honest woman must recognise herself in Anna Karenina' – Tolstoy's novel *Anna Karenina* (1877) is the story of a woman who abandons marriage and child for her lover (see p. 15, l. 10).

P.13.

1 'catalepsy': a seizure or trance in which consciousness is suspended (for other tranced moments, see p. 4, l. 1; p. 17, l. 2).

French café gossip is contrasted with the silence of Germans.

2–7   Subaqueous: (constructed) under water; this passage echoes the preface to *Madeleine*, where 'Life' (or as here, 'Experience') is the material out of which Art is gradually formed.

9–10   With these lines, the description of the Grands Boulevards comes to an end, suggesting, perhaps, that the life of the Boulevards provides raw material needing to be formed into speech or words, if it is to become art ('coming to' could mean coming back to consciousness). Lines 8–10 themselves burst into 'vastness' after the six narrow lines that precede them (see also Tennyson's poem, 'Vastness').

11–26   1 May is celebrated a Labour Day in France, but in 1919 there was a general strike in Paris, with violent clashes between the authorities and the workers, some of whom marched with knives between their teeth (Hausser 726; MacMillan 273). The vertical lettering emphasises the disruption of normal order, representing the line of marchers, and possibly the stems of the (absent) lily of the valley, usually sold on 1 May, to give to friends or sweethearts as bringer of luck (p. 7, l. 22).

P.14.

10–12   The struggle between the chaos of life and the structure of art (p. 13, ll. 2–8) now becomes a 'ritual fight' between two virgins, as the year progresses from 'The wicked April moon' (*la lune rousse*) to the month of May, sacred to the Virgin Mary. The April moon is the lunar month after Easter, characterised by cold, harsh winds that seem to scorch (*roussir*) the new growth. '[H]er sweet body' could be that of Paris.

13   Punning on the English expression, 'the silence of the grave', *la grève* is the strike (on 1 May), with a further underlying wordplay, since *la grève* means the river bank – the place de *Grève* (now,

place de l'Hôtel de Ville) being where Parisian workers assembled to *faire la grève*, or go on strike.

17–18 'the mysterious island gardens' seem to be those of the Carrousel, running from the Arc de Triomphe du Carrousel down to the Tuileries.

19–21 The Seine winds westwards through the centre of Paris, reaching the sea at Le Havre. 'Ruminating', literally, chewing the cud, and thus recycling or recirculating, also suggests the river's passage through the fertile dairy-farming province of Normandy. Initially associated with the underworld (p. 3, l. 10), the Seine is here (and later, p. 21, l. 8) associated with the Freudian unconscious, which increasingly asserts itself as dreams (p. 14, l. 21, and see p. 16, l. 15; p. 19, l. 15), anticipated by the melting of the Louvre (p. 14, l. 15; compare p. 16, ll. 16–20).

22 'King-fishers', small, bright blue diving birds.

P.15.

1–2 Paris now becomes a sequence of pictures: the two-dimensional (as at p. 20, l. 20) silhouette of the Eiffel Tower (a favourite subject for artists) is 'etched' (engraved, black on white), while the soldiers encamped in the Tuileries are drawn in coloured chalk, and the page ends with (imaginary) oil paintings.

3–7 'The *Poilus*' (literally 'hairy'), French World War 1 soldiers in blue uniforms, with *Terre de Sienne* (burnt Sienna, reddish brown) packs, around the 'gray sphinx' look like the chalk sketches, 'edited' (i.e., published) in the rue des Pyramides, a street where souvenirs are sold. The combination of sphinx and pyramids recalls Napoleon's campaign in Egypt, as well as World War 1 operations in Egypt (MacMillan 382–3, 401).

8–13 'Désœuvrement' (idleness, lack of occupation, suffered by demobilised soldiers) suggests Vronsky; 'Apprehension' suggests

(39)

Anna, the lovers at the centre of Tolstoy's *Anna Karenina* (p. 12, l. 25). In part 4, they wake from similar dreams of a sinister Russian peasant (a 'mujik'), perhaps unconsciously anticipating the Bolshevik Revolution (1917).

14–17   Even the most violent and calamitous moments of history can be transformed into the tranquillity of art. Clio, the Greek muse of history, becomes a French painter, stilling the watery flux of life. Shadrach et al. were cast by Nebuchadnezzar into the fiery furnace (Daniel 3.12–30), but in art they become 'motionless and plastic'.

18–21   'Manet's *Massacres* . . .' a series of paintings imagined as hanging in the Louvre, depicting violent moments of French history: Manet (1832–83) is imagined portraying the massacres of 'les journées de Juin' (days of June 1848 when protesters were rounded up, disarmed, and killed by the army); David (1748–1825), as painting the taking of the Bastille (14 July 1789, the beginning of the French Revolution); while Nicolas Poussin (1594–1665), as depicting the uprisings of the Fronde (1649, 1652) (see *Madeleine*, 11–12). Pages 13–15 of the Hogarth edition survive in a proof, corrected by HM. Here the first imaginary painting was originally 'Cézanne's *Quatorze Juillet*' – apparently altered because its subject, '14 July', was too close to David's. 'Manet's *Massacres des Jours de Juin*' was substituted. Manet actually painted *The Execution of Maximilian* (1867) and the executions of May 1871. HM's revisions produce a historical sequence, running from the strike of 1 May 1919, back through the risings of 1848, 1789 and 1652, to illustrate French political resistance.

22–3   Like Clio (but not like Vronsky), the Virgin has been busy – creating business for (and later actually window-dressing) Paris's three largest and best-known department stores – les Galéries Lafayette, le Bon Marché (see p. 7, l. 11), and la Samaritaine.

P.16.

1–2   According to HM's notes to *Paris*, during Lent, depart-
ment store windows displayed wax models dressed for First
Communion in white veils and ties (knots of ribbon) as 'bait', to
encourage young girls to participate by showing the pretty
clothes they could wear. But these 'Waxen Pandoras' are also
'bait' in a further sense, since (according to Hesiod, lines 80–82)
Pandora was sent by Zeus to tempt Prometheus and punish him
from stealing fire from the gods. Pandora was modelled from
clay (not wax), and carried a jar containing all the evils of the
world. When she opened it, they all flew out into the world,
except Hope (HM's own name), left inside the jar.

3   *Catéchisme de Persévérance*, a popular nineteenth-century
Catholic manual by Jean-Joseph Gaume. The decrees of the
'Seven Œcumenical Councils' (Nicea I, AD 325–Nicea II, AD
787) embody the central doctrines of Christianity; 'format'
means 'size'; *Bibliothèque Rose*, a series of books for girls pub-
lished by Hachette.

6–7   'First communion'. Prometheus has swallowed the 'bait'
of Pandora, or the communion wafer, or is excited by the First
Communicants.

8–10   'Petits Lycéens', little high-school children. 'Por-no-gra-
phie', spelled out as if for children, is a Greek word meaning, lit-
erally, writings about prostitution; 'pigmy brides' are miniature
brides of Christ. 'Pigmy' is a Greek word for the forearm or fist,
anticipating the cannibal imagery that follows ('teknophagiai',
the eating of children, is discussed by JH in *Themis* 248–9).

11–12   'Little Saint Hugh' (not an actual saint), according to
anti-Semitic legend, a child murdered by Jews in Lincoln (1255).
Chaucer's *Prioress's Tale* tells a similar story. By eating the body of

Christ (the Jew) at first communion, the children 'avenge' St Hugh's murder.

13   A photographic studio in Paris? A peepshow?

17   Périgord is a rural region in south-western France, part of the poem's tour of provinces.

18–20   The Louvre is the great palace at the heart of Paris, now an art gallery; the Ritz is a hotel at 15, Place Vendôme; the Palais-Royal[e] is opposite the Louvre; the Hôtel de Ville, the Paris Mairie (or town hall), is east of the Louvre on the rue de Rivoli. All are solid, indeed massive buildings, that could only appear 'light and frail' in a rising atmosphere of dreams (see p. 14, l. 15).

21–2   'junketing', feasting, merrymaking. Masks and dominoes are carnival disguises (the domino is the cloak to go with the mask), typically worn by the aristocracy, but here by 'citizens', thus anticipating the Revolution.

23   'On the occasion of the marriage of Monsieur le Dauphin', the marriage celebrations of the future Louis XVI to Marie-Antoinette. In the course of these (30–31 May 1770) a display of fireworks created a stampede in which several hundred people were crushed to death or pushed into the river.

P.17.

1–3   The Hôtel de l'Elysée, 3, rue de Beaune, where HM stayed in Paris and apparently wrote this poem, was a hotel in the modern sense, as well as in the older sense of a grand town house, formerly the property of Mme du Deffand, famous for her *salon*. 'Tranced' (p. 4, l. 1, and perhaps p. 5, l. 6), trance states, and the automatic writing they generated, were to fascinate the Surrealists. It is possible that the whole poem, flickering between 'real' and imagined Paris sights, was generated by this 'tranced' moment of gazing out of the window (Keatsian 'magic casements, opening on the foam / Of perilous seas, in fairy lands forlorn').

4   'Hawkers . . . liturgically', street peddlars . . . in the style of a church service.

5–6   'Triptolemos', a legendary king of Eleusis who founded the Mysteries and taught men agriculture (including how to make bread). As a baby (wrapped in swaddling clothes that make him 'loaf-shaped'), he was loved by Demeter (Ceres), probably identified with the 'women in black shawls'.

7–8   'Workmen in pale blue', wearing denim overalls; 'Barrows' belong to street vendors displaying their wares.

14   Ovid, Roman poet and storyteller (43 BC–AD 17), was exiled to Tomis on the Black Sea, but not a 'thrall' (i.e., slave) in Fairyland (as was the narrator of Keats's poem, 'La Belle Dame Sans Merci'). The resulting 'lost romance' is imagined as having inspired Italian painters, as their 'guild-secret', peculiar to their craft.

21–2   Three landmarks of seventeenth-century Paris to the north and east, by 1919 in a state of disrepair, and thus 'exquisitely dying' (see p. 5, l. 2).

P.18.

1–4   Quiet was expected for the dying. The eight bars of music are marked 'dim—in—u-en-do' (growing softer) to 'ppp', pianissimo, very quiet indeed. The melancholy aria is 'Lascia ch'io pianga', from Handel's opera *Rinaldo* (1711), 'Let me weep for my cruel fate, and let me sigh for my liberty' (recalling Ovid's misery in exile?).

5–6   The beautiful church of Saint Thomas d'Aquin (begun 1688, completed in 1766) stands near the end of the rue de Beaune. L'impasse des Deux Anges (the blind alley of the two angels) is close by. The angels may be linked with Jacob (see Genesis 28.12, or 32.24–9), though 'two angels' are particularly connected with Lot and the destruction of the cities of the plain (Genesis 19.1–17), punished by God for homosexuality (see Cocteau, 28–9, 47; 45, 66). The name of the 'impasse' might also suggest lesbianism. It was close to Natalie Barney's house (at 20, rue Jacob) and is referred to in Djuna Barnes's *The Ladies' Almanack* (1928).

6–8 'Impasse', a blind alley, also suggests 'deadlock' (both in French and English), and 'impassive' (i.e., blank or inexpressive, *impassible*). The French expression for walls without windows, *murs aveugles* (blind walls) may have suggested the comparison with blind dogs. The ghosts, watched by the 'impassive windows' (compare p. 7, l. 24), introduce a pageant of the city's famous dead.

12 Sebastopol, port on the Black Sea, besieged and eventually captured (1856) by English and French troops (greatly aided by Algerians, the 'Zouaves') during the Crimean War, and commemorated by a street name and a métro station.

13–20 The memorial plaque for the playwright (1622–73) on his house at 40, rue de Richelieu, on the Right Bank, north of the Louvre (see p. 10, l. 1; p. 12, l. 5). 'The dying seventeenth century' is followed by the memorial plaque for the Enlightenment philosopher, Voltaire (1694–1778), who died at no. 1, rue de Beaune, next door to or even part of HM's hotel.

P.19.

1–4 Chateaubriand, Romantic poet and memoirist (1768–1848), died close by, at 118–20 rue du Bac, with the blind Mme Récamier at his bedside (p. 6, ll. 3–4). These writers typify three different centuries, and three different French styles.

6–7 'Paradise' is almost an anagram of 'Paris' and 'dies'. Les

Champs Elysées, Paris's most famous avenue, means 'the Elysian fields' in classical literature, the home of the dead.

8   The French critic Charles Saint-Beuve (1804–69) was the friend and rival of the poet and novelist Victor Hugo (1802–85), and the lover of his wife Adèle. The Pont Neuf ('New Bridge', now the oldest, completed 1604) would take Saint-Beuve from his house on the Left Bank to the Right (where the Hugos lived, at 6, place de Vosges).

9–12   The duc de la Rochefoucauld (1613–80), author of *Maximes* (1664) and a close friend of Mme de Lafayette (1634–93), author of *La Princesse de Clèves* (1678). He passes Saint-Beuve on the Pont Neuf as he crosses to the Left Bank to visit Mme Lafayette in the rue Ferou. They cannot see each other, perhaps because of the centuries between them, but the duc had figured in Saint-Beuve's great study of the seventeenth century, *Port-Royal* (1840–59). The *salon d'automne* exhibited avant-garde painting; it was originally formed by a group of Fauvists and Post-Impressionists in 1903 (Shattuck 61).

14   'It's close, sultry' (literally, heavy, as in 'Heavy sweet going', p. 16, l. 16).

16   'Benediction', a Catholic service. 'Notre-Dame-de-Champs' (Our Lady of the fields) is one of the oldest churches in Paris; formerly standing in fields on Montparnasse, it was rebuilt in 1876. Its métro station is south of rue du Bac on the Nord-Sud line, between Port-Royal (p. 22, l. 10) and the garden of the nuns of St Vincent de Paul, on the rue de Babylone (now the Jardin Catherine Laboure).

18–21   The Virgin wears the elaborately starched headdress of the nuns of St Vincent de Paul (winged like the Roman helmets of p. 10, l. 20) and probably sits in their convent garden (see above), where the west wall would have been covered with plum and apricot trees, and there are still box hedges. The Holy Ghost descended as a dove, and 'cooing' and '(dove)-cots' are common to babies and doves (compare Cocteau 22: 'Dieu roucoule au sommet des arbres').

22 'The Seven Stages', possibly half of the fourteen Stations of the Cross, performed on Good Friday, representing Christ's final sufferings; 'cut in box', either means carved in boxwood, or from topiary (pruning box hedges into shapes). Churches display branches of box during Easter week.

P.20.

1–3 White ('Madonna') lilies, the Virgin's flower. Votive offerings result from a religious promise. The Jap(anese) convert is the painter L.T. Foujita (1886–1968), who painted pictures of the Virgin and Child in soft colours (1917–18), often in shapes resembling bulbs.

4–6 'troubadour', Provençal travelling minstrel. The cult of courtly love voiced in troubadour poetry was linked with the cult of the Virgin; 'her', i.e., to her. 'Venial sins' are lesser ones than Deadly Sins (at p. 8, l. 12; p. 21, ll. 20–1).

7–8 The garden wall becomes the evening sky, hung with the plums of Paradise, where wasps never fret (eat away) the fruit; on the Solférino bridge, however, people look like flies, nibbling into the apricot (coloured) sky (p. 20, ll. 16–18).

9–10; 13 'Freedom!' 'The Press!' names of evening newspapers shouted by street vendors.

11–12 'Petit-Palais', built for the 1900 World Exhibition, west of the Place de Concorde, and perhaps just visible from a high west-facing window at the end of the rue de Beaune. At sunset in the Algerian desert the 'muezzin' gives the Muslim call to prayer.

17–21 'Fiacres', light, horse-drawn four-wheeled cabs. Looking westward, HM might just have seen figures on the old Pont Solférino (demolished 1961), silhouetted like flies against the celestial (heavenly) evening haze; 'tippetted pelisse', a fur-collared cloak. Louis-Philippe, 'the citizen king', reigned 1830–48, when portraits in silhouette, cut from black paper, were in vogue.

22–3 The Quais are the streets along the banks of the Seine, where the 'bouquinistes' (box-owners, booksellers) sell their wares from green boxes, which they lock up at night.

P.21.

1 Paris has twenty *arrondissements* (administrative districts). The VIIme lies immediately south of the river, on the Left Bank, and includes the rue de Beaune; like the neighbouring VIme, this was an up-market address, known as the 'Faubourg Saint-Germain'.

4 'Hyperbórean', northern. The poem prepares to move up to Montmartre, in the north of Paris.

7 'Ramparts', mounds built for defence. The Louvre was initially built as a fortress (in 1200). Here ramparts keep the river, and perhaps the unconscious, at bay.

8–9 Sigmund Freud (1856–1939), Viennese theorist of sexuality and the unconscious, dredges the river, associated with rising dreams (p. 14, ll. 19–22). The combination of Freud and electricity evokes modern life. Paris had had electrically lit advertisements from 1912 (Higonnet 145, 358, and compare 'Contrastes': 'Il pleut les globes electriques', Blaise Cendrars, *Poésies Complètes*, ed. Claude Leroy [Paris: Denoël, 2001], p. 71).

10–12 Taxis line up on the page, as they do on the streets.

15 'their meat', perhaps their clients (see p. 3, l. 4; the opening themes are now replayed).

16   'padre', 'Father' (a Catholic priest) strikes at the Moulin Rouge (literally, the Red Windmill), Paris's most famous cabaret show (on the Place Blanche, Montmartre). To tilt with windmills is to make an ineffectual attack (from *Don Quixote*).

17   Black music notes become African-American musicians playing jazz; 'syncopation', shifting of the regular musical beat, as in jazz. Today this sentence is disturbingly racist, although the black musicians, like the lesbians in the following lines, introduce a liberating discourse of racial and sexual alterity. Jazz was brought to Paris by black US army bands at the end of World War 1, and was fashionable in Montmartre (Higonnet 341).

19; p. 22, 1   Literally, all the cards (or maps) work with, walk with or go out with a match, but the exact meaning is hard to decide. It might refer to packs of cards given out in cafés, with boxes of matches, but 'cartes' was also slang for prostitutes, and an 'allumette' might be a sexual tease, or even a penis. A song refrain?

20   Fifty pairs of glasses, designed to correct American 'astigmatism' (a sight defect that prevents focusing), reflect a (leg) show saucily entitled 'the Masque of the Seven Deadly Sins' (see p. 8, l. 12), a pseudo-religious title for a secular event, perhaps suggesting a further clash between the Virgin and 'The wicked April moon'.

22–3   Stage performers, like courtesans, were often supposed lesbian, and lesbianism was fashionable in Paris at this time (Higonnet 112–13). The spelling 'gurls' may indicate an American accent, but 'girls' was also French slang both for lesbians and chorus girls.

P.22.

2   Dawn brings the poem's time scheme of a single day to a close.

3   Paul Verlaine (1844–96), lyric poet and decadent, fell in love with the precocious Arthur Rimbaud (1854–91), author of

'L'Alchimie du verbe' (a section of his prose poem *Une Saison en Enfer*). 'Alchemy', the transformation of base metal into gold, is also a figure for the coming of dawn. 'Absynthe' [unusually spelled with a 'y'] is a powerful green spirit distilled from wormwood to which Verlaine was addicted. Picasso's 1903 painting, *Portrait du poète Cornuti, ou l'Absinthe* is a form of homage to Verlaine. Algerian tobacco was used to roll cheap cigarettes and joints (p. 3, l. 3; p. 12, l. 4).

8–9 Raymond Poincaré was president of France (1913–20). The poem here rocks between homosexuality and heterosexuality (the marriage bed, birth), between couples and single lives.

10 'Port-Royal', maternity hospital on the Left Bank, formerly a convent associated with Jansenism, a movement within the French seventeenth-century church persecuted by the authorities (and the focus of Saint-Beuve's study, *Port-Royal*). In chapter XVI of *Madeleine*, Madeleine visits the Abbaye, whose mistress, Mère Agnès Arnauld, is a portrait of JH (157).

11 This line suggests Duncan Grant's painting *Le Crime et le Châtiment* (ca. 1909), especially since Dostoevsky's novel (1866) was usually translated *Crime et Châtiment*. HM knew Grant, and may have known that the painting showed Marjorie Strachey reading that novel.

13 'Les Halles', until the late 1960s, Paris's main food market, rebuilt of wrought iron and glass (1866).

15 'I salute you Paris full of grace', echoing the Catholic prayer 'Ave Maria', 'Je vous salue Marie pleine de grace' (see Dedication; Cocteau 82: 'Je vous salue pleine de grace . . . o sainte mère').

16 The poem ends with the constellation of Ursa Major, the great she-bear, part of the private code between HM and JH, who sometimes signed off letters to HM with this star sign in reverse.

19　The original Hogarth Press edition mistakenly printed the poem's completion date as '1916'; Virginia Woolf hand-corrected most of the copies by writing '9' over the '6'.

On the final page, HM makes a further highly original gesture by providing a set of notes to her admittedly difficult poem. Though not without precedent (Pope had annotated his 'Dunciad'), it was unusual for an author to annotate her own text thus. Brief and fragmentary though her notes are, they offer a fresh perspective on the poem, and incidentally anticipate T. S. Eliot's use of notes in *The Waste Land* (1922).

JULIA BRIGGS, 2007

Works Cited

Cocteau, Jean. *Oeuvres Poétiques Completes*, ed. Michel Decaudin. Paris: Gallimard, 1999.

Cendrars, Blaise. *Poésies Completes*, ed. Claude Leroy. Paris: Denoel, 2001.

Harrison, Jane. *Themis: A Study of the Social Origins of Greek Religion*. 1912; London: Merlin Press, 1989.

Hausser, Elisabeth. *Paris au jour le jour: les évenéments vus par la Presse, 1900–1919*. Paris: Les Editions de Minuit, 1968.

Higonnet, Patrice. *Paris, Capital of the World*, trans. Arthur Goldhammer. Cambridge: Harvard University Press, 2002.

MacMillan, Margaret. *Paris 1919: Six Months that Changed the World*. New York: Random House, 2002.

Mirrlees, Hope. *Madeleine, One of Love's Jansenists*. London: W. Collins, 1919.

Shattuck, Roger. *The Banquet Years, The Origins of the Avant-Garde in France: 1885 to World War I*. London: Jonathan Cape, 1969.

ADDENDUM

HM made six substantive changes to *Paris* for its republication in the *Virginia Woolf Quarterly* in 1973.

The following lines were omitted: p. 9, ll. 1–5; p. 15, ll. 22–3; p. 16, ll. 1–2 and p. 16, ll. 7–12.

p. 18, l. 11   'Masses' was replaced by 'dirges'.

p. 19, ll. 18–22; p. 20, ll. 1–8   These thirteen lines, commencing 'The Virgin . . .' and ending with '. . . of Paradise', were omitted and replaced by the following fourteen lines:

> The Virgin sits in her garden;
> She wears the blue habit and the
> white head-dress of the nuns of
> > St. Vincent of Paul.
>
> The fourteen stations of the Cross are
> carved in box;
> Lilies bloom, blue, green and pink,
> The bulbs were votive offerings
> From a converted Japanese. An angelic troubadour
> Sings her songs of her Son's courtly love.
> Upon the wall of sunset sky wasps never fret
> The plums of Paradise.
>
> Upon the wall of sunset-sky wasps never fret
> > The plums of Paradise.
>
> > [*La Liberté La Presse!, etc.*]

p. 21, l. 17   'Niggers' was replaced by the more acceptable term 'Negroes'.

The following changes have been made to this edition.

p. 11, l. 24   'Grand' to 'Grands'
p. 19, l. 10   'leisuerly' to 'leisurely'
p. 23, note to p. 15   'Laffayette' to 'Lafayette'

SANDEEP PARMAR, 2020

AFTERWORD

In the hundred years since Hope Mirrlees's *Paris: A Poem* was published by Leonard and Virginia Woolf's Hogarth Press there have been several attempts to reintroduce it to readers. Mirrlees herself denied a request from Leonard to republish the poem in 1946; later, she grudgingly allowed the *Virginia Woolf Quarterly* to do so (with 'blasphemous' portions rewritten); that journal, based in California, folded after just three issues. In 2007, decades after Mirrlees's death, the Woolf scholar Julia Briggs anthologised *Paris* in a doorstopper American compendium of women's writing, *Gender in Modernism*, alongside extensive notes that are reproduced here. That same year, the London-based little magazine, *The Wolf*, printed *Paris* for the first time in the UK since 1920. Subsequently, Pegana Press, a specialist American publisher of mostly fantasy writers, brought out a costly collector's volume. In 2011, my own critical edition of Mirrlees's *Collected Poems* set *Paris* within her wider poetic *oeuvre* and her life, drawn mostly from her newly discovered literary archive. More recent are the Hurst Street Press lovingly hand-stitched, limited-edition artist books of *Paris*, each with individually marbled covers. The poem's small-press publication history and afterlife – most of the reappraisals have emerged from feminist modernist revisions to the canon – contribute to its cult, marginal status. A critical reappraisal of *Paris* is building, albeit within the confines of academic study, where speculative narratives and heroic figures constellate an ever-crowded sky. One way or another, *Paris* has evaded a majority of readers. The hope of this edition is to make Mirrlees's remarkable, singular poem widely available in print for the first time so that it may find the audience it deserves.

Paris is as worthy a long poem as its better-known comparators such as T. S. Eliot's *The Waste Land*, whose publication two years later, in 1922, the American poet William Carlos Williams would recall as the aesthetic equivalent of an 'atom bomb'. Like *The Waste Land*, *Paris* responds to the trauma of World War I and the bewildering occasion of peacetime. By invoking myth, history and modernity across a mourning cityscape, Mirrlees reasons with the ruins of her civilisation. And while some might argue, without historical evidence, that Eliot must have benefited from *Paris*'s example, Mirrlees's compellingly innovative poem, like the work of many modernist women writers, stands in the shadow of its male-authored contemporaries. It is too easy to simply write off these neglected texts as collateral damage to the canonisation of male genius. Likewise it is not enough to account for their absence without carefully stripping away assumptions about cultural value that accrue around (or fail to adhere to) a literary text. To appreciate *Paris* in its full context we must understand its unique moment and the life of the woman who wrote it, being mindful of but not magnetised by the poem's fated obscurity. Importantly, we must also be guided by our enthusiasm as readers as we cross wildly impossible distances in a single day in Paris, 1919. We must be prepared to be carried away by the poem's sensuous surfaces, to step freshly into a city we think we know, from experience or reputation, changed by the poet's vivid imagination and desire. Only then will we be able to appreciate the passion and allure with which Mirrlees's extraordinary – or, as Virginia Woolf put it, 'obscure, indecent, and brilliant' – poem was written.

*

Among Mirrlees's notes in her archive, a single sentence sums up the year *Paris* was written: '1919 Return to Paris in Spring and spend some months.' No manuscript for *Paris* has survived save three proof pages with handwritten corrections (likely made in April 1920). Little information about the poem's composition emerges from her correspondence. In place of these details, we must consider the wider frame of the life of Hope Mirrlees. Born in 1887 in Kent into a close-knit, upper-middle-class family of Scottish industrialists with ties to South African sugar production, Mirrlees studied classics at Newnham College, Cambridge, from 1910 to 1913. There she was taught by the scholar Jane Ellen Harrison whose work on ancient Greek religion, art and ritual would shape Mirrlees's intellectual and aesthetic sensibility thereafter. Despite the considerable, nearly forty-year age difference between them, Harrison and Mirrlees became close companions. After 1915 they spent months at a time in Paris studying Russian while Mirrlees was researching for a novel and Harrison wrote, translated and received treatment for a heart condition. Following Harrison's retirement from Newnham in 1922 they resettled in Paris until 1926, before moving back to London to live in Mecklenburgh Square where Harrison died from leukaemia in April 1928. Not even a full decade on from *Paris*, and with three novels under her belt, Mirrlees found herself disconsolate and anchorless. Two years later she converted to Roman Catholicism, superimposing deep religious feeling onto her love for Harrison. During World War II, she left London to live with her mother in Surrey where her friend T. S. Eliot (a connection developed largely after Harrison's death) frequently boarded with them during the Blitz. And whilst Mirrlees continued to work on various writing projects – some realised, others not – she did not publish again for almost forty years. She died, aged ninety-one, in

August 1978 at the Thames Bank nursing home in Goring-on-Thames.

Harrison's influence on Mirrlees was, in her own words, a kind of 're-creation', but the collaborative nature of their relationship was mutually supportive. Harrison's early letters to Mirrlees are peppered with recommended reading, eventually giving way to palpable intimacy and musings on the inner life of their totemic teddy bear, 'The Old One', who was a kind of shared husband. In notes for an uncompleted biography of Harrison, Mirrlees claimed that Harrison had learned a great deal from the way she 'attacked the whole of a civilisation, instead of just a part of it' in her writing. For Harrison, Mirrlees's presence was invigorating and gave her a new lease on life, to paraphrase her own words. From Mirrlees's novels and poetry to Harrison's tracts on religion and art, both women tirelessly and uniquely rethought the pattern of modern and ancient human society. Harrison's intellectual fingerprints are all over *Paris* from the fourth word, 'holophrase', to the ritual Spirit of the Year figure of renewal, to the final sign of Ursa Major, dotted in asterisks in their published writings and postcards to each other. The constellation of the great bear was just one among many signs they shared between them in a private, encoded language.

*

Spring 1919 was quiet and cold. The Peace Conference was underway but a stillness replaced the anxiety of Zeppelin attacks and the war misery of preceding years. The Seine flooded, inching its way towards the Left Bank rue de Beaune where the two women kept rooms at the Hôtel de l'Elysée from April to July. The weather put a dampener on the First of May demonstrations, according to a letter from Harrison to Gilbert Murray: 'Riots were expected but all fell flat and it was like an English Sunday – traffic stopped shops shut and nothing doing.'

The heaviness of water, like the weight of history and the invisible war dead, are conjured by the poem's consciousness: 'Il fait lourd, / The dreams have reached my waist'. At other moments, the poem smashes dramatic unities and leaps from Left to Right Bank like Nijinsky or accelerates with the dynamism of Futurism, juxtaposing the ancient world ('Black-figured vases in Etruscan tombs') with the technology of electricity, the nightlife of Montmartre and the allure of modern advertising. *Paris* has an extraordinary way of conveying many superimposed cities at once, implying that, like a ruin, the modern city is merely the aggregate of newness destroyed in perpetuity.

Paris: A Poem appeared in May 1920 and was only the fifth book from the Hogarth Press, following on the heels of stories by the Woolfs, Katherine Mansfield, a privately circulated poetry pamphlet by Leonard's brother Cecil Nathan Sidney Woolf, and poems by Eliot. Reviews were few and divided: *The Athenaeum* praised Mirrlees's adoption of 'the idiom of the younger French poets' like Blaise Cendrars and called it 'immensely literary and immensely accomplished'. Indeed, Mirrlees benefited from reading the work of her French contemporaries, such as Guillaume Apollinaire's 'Zone', and she herself would later point to the influence of Jean Cocteau's *Le Cap de Bonne-Espérance*. Mirrlees would have had access to the original, although it was translated into English by Jean Hugo and published by Ezra Pound in *The Little Review* in 1921, and very likely influenced Eliot's *The Waste Land* (which may account for similarities with *Paris*). Resemblances to Cocteau's controversial poem include the appearance of St John of Patmos, the aperitif Byrrh, as well as varied typography and concrete form controlling the poem's energy like a spigot.

But not everyone was impressed. The *Times Literary Supplement* reviewer found it 'spluttering and incoherent', a 'futurist trick to give an ensemble of the sensations offered to a pilgrim through Paris'. In short, Mirrlees's tricks of type were unworthy of 'the art of poetry'. Such a conventional view is hardly surprising at a time when the poetic innovators of British modernism relied so heavily on European models veering demonstrably from formal English verse. Unlike other 'difficult' poems, *Paris* would not be championed by the capacious machinery of modernist production – editors, patrons, fellow avant-garde poets did not take up her cause, nor did she seek their company in the cafés and salons of Paris or London. We know that Mirrlees's friendship with Gertrude Stein did not give her entrée into these circles, though she visited Stein and Alice B. Toklas's home on the rue de Fleurus and they kept up a lively correspondence. It was not until much later in Mirrlees's life, when she and Eliot became close friends in the 1940s, that he nurtured and eventually published her extraordinary biography of the antiquary Sir Robert Bruce Cotton, a decades-long project which Eliot referred to in letters as her 'Penelope's Web'. Whether by circumstance or choice, Mirrlees's poetic career was over before it began.

What new life might this poem find, in this already weary century? What might it teach us now, as we commemorate world wars with definite beginnings and endings in this, our age of never-ending war? Can we walk with Mirrlees through her beloved Paris today, knowing perhaps little of her obscure and complex references, but feeling instinctively the energy, desire and regret of our own ever-modernising lives? This poem is, indeed, an ensemble of sensations, embodied sometimes by a singular figure who appears, at odd whiles, our Baudelairean woman of the crowd, our *flâneuse*. *Paris* instructs us how to see and listen to the gait of the present.

But it also startlingly brings to life a city lost to the past: the voice of an old nun chanting masses, American servicemen at jazz clubs, hawkers on the street, the sounds of newly opened métro trains and the glare of advertisements for exotic colonial products, the famous and nameless dead, as well as the living who have endured tragedy and survived, who must now inhabit this great metropolis side by side with those they mourn.

SANDEEP PARMAR, 2020

This edition of *Paris: A Poem* by Hope Mirrlees
is based upon the design of the first edition
printed in Caslon Old Face type on the Hogarth Press
by Leonard and Virginia Woolf in Richmond, Surrey, in 1920,
and sewn by hand, in a print run of 175 copies.